The
✝rue
Cross Bearers

The

✝rue

Cross Bearers

Rufus M. Parker

The True Cross Bearers
© 2019
Rufus M. Parker

ALL RIGHTS RESERVED

No portion of this publication may be reproduced, stored in any electronic system, or transmitted in any form or by any means, electronic, mechanical, photocopy, recording, or otherwise, without written permission from the author. Brief quotations may be used in literary reviews.

All Scripture quotations herein are from the Authorized King James Version of the Bible.

**For Information Contact:
okipreacher@gmail.com**

And he said to them all,
If any man will come after me,
let him deny himself,
and take up his cross daily,
and follow me.
(Luke 9:23)

*And whosoever doth not
bear his cross,
and come after me,
cannot be my disciple.*
(Luke 14:27)

Acknowledgments

I must start by thanking my awesome and most wonderful wife, Pam. For forty-two years, you have inspired me to do my best. Thanks for always being willing to stop what you are doing to help me whenever I need you. You display what this book is all about.

To my daughter Martha, son Bob, daughter-in-law Janet, and my pastor, Paul Dennis, for giving me advice with this work. Thanks to each of you for your comments, corrections, and directions. I would like to thank my dear friend and pastor, Tony McCall, for his outstanding artwork and cover design. Tony, thank you for your many years of friendship and kindness; you are the best at this.

To my wonderful armor bearers, Denny and Kathy Thompson, thank you so very much for your daily prayer covering. In so many ways, I feel your prayers are what energize me to keep writing. I would also like to thank Sister Bethany Sledge for her editing and layout. You always do such fantastic work.

Finally, but in no way last, I want to thank the Lord Jesus Christ, as without Him I can do nothing. I pray that this book will be an inspiration to all who read it, and that each of you will always be true cross bearers of the Lord Jesus Christ.

Rufus M. Parker,
a true cross bearer

Table of Contents

Introduction 13
I. Compassion 19
II. Resistance 27
III. Obedience 35
IV. Submission 45
V. Servanthood 55

Introduction

A story relates that a man came to Jesus to complain that the cross he was required to carry was too heavy. Jesus led him into a vast room with many crosses along the walls. He told the man to place his cross among the others and look around to see if he thought he could carry another one.

After spending much time going around the room and looking at all the available crosses, the man finally decided on one. He said to Jesus, "I think I have found a cross I will be able to carry. I will take this one."

Jesus smiled and replied, "But that's the one you brought with you!"

The True Cross Bearers

Throughout the Gospels, Jesus taught many things by parables (a simple story used to illustrate a moral or spiritual lesson) to bring about understanding and enlightenment and to establish spiritual principles. What exactly did Jesus mean when He said, *And whosoever doth not bear his cross, and come after me, cannot be my disciple* (Luke 14:27)? What was the significance of the cross? Why did the apostle Paul preach about the cross, and why must we preach and teach it? Why did Jesus select the cross as one of the methods in making us His disciples?

Were His words factual or prophetic? Answer: a bit of both. Was He stating that we must literally die on a cross like Him or we cannot be His disciples, or was there a deeper meaning? I find that His words always have more than a surface meaning. This, I believe, is why some are perplexed about what they read in the Bible. They read and hear but do not understand. They see but do not perceive. They fail to obtain the Scripture's deeper meaning. I am sure you have heard

Introduction

the old statement, "I know you think you understood what I said, but I'm not sure you understood what I meant."

The apostle Paul wrote, *For the preaching of the cross is to them that perish foolishness; but unto us which are saved it is the power of God* (1 Corinthians 1:18). He explained that the cross will not make sense to some. However, to those who have been born again of the water and the Spirit, living a holy, separated life, the cross holds deeper meaning. It brought salvation, eternal life, empowerment!

If we were to die on a cross as Christ did, how could we accomplish the work He sends us to do or achieve what He desires to fulfill through us? I would like us to focus on five areas that I believe represent the cross Jesus has called us to carry. We all should ask ourselves, "What will I need to do to bear it daily, and how can I follow His example while doing it?" Hopefully, we will learn to put into action the things the cross represents so we may become His true disciples.

***And of some
have compassion,
making a difference.***
(Jude 1:22)

I. Compassion

Compassion: Showing sympathy, empathy, concern, kindness, and consideration. The first step in carrying our cross daily is *compassion*, which literally means "to suffer together." Some researchers of emotion explain compassion as the feeling that arises when we are confronted with another's suffering and feel the motivation to relieve his suffering. Compassion is one of the qualities a Christian must possess. It should be at the heart of all we do. **It has been stated that if we lose our compassion, we lose what it is to be human.**

Jeremiah, during his lamentation for Israel, wrote, *It is of the LORD'S mercies that we are not consumed, because his compassions fail not. They are new every morning: great is thy faithfulness* (Lamentations 3:22-23). He called Israel to understand God's compassion for them. Although they were suffering, God's compassion was still there. He desired to alleviate their suffering. Notice, God's compassions fail not; they are new every morning. **If we are true cross bearers, our compassions must never fail. They, too, must be renewed every morning!**

We must be able to see the hurt and despondency in others around us and be ready to help alleviate their pain. As Jude wrote, *Of some have compassion, making a difference.* We cannot make a difference in others' lives if we do not take up our cross daily and follow Christ. Jesus was often moved with compassion when He saw the people as sheep without a shepherd (Matthew 9:36). Compassion was a component of His DNA. As it flowed in His veins, it must flow through ours as well. We must have compassion and make a difference.

The apostle Paul said to the church at Galatia, *Brethren, if a man be overtaken in a fault, ye which are spiritual,*

Compassion

restore such an one in the spirit of meekness; considering thyself, lest thou also be tempted. . . . As we have therefore opportunity, let us do good unto all men, especially unto them who are of the household of faith (Galatians 6:1, 10). Compassion does not mean that I must agree with you because you are in a predicament or negative situation. It may be your fault you are there, but **compassion sees a remorseful and hurting heart and reaches out to alleviate the suffering.** Compassion does not see race or color. It reaches across all racial lines and barriers and sees the need to help.

Compassion feels another's hurt by putting on the other person's shoes, so to speak. Compassion moved Jesus when He saw the multitudes as sheep having no shepherd. He was so moved with compassion, when He saw the tears of Mary, Lazarus's sister, and the Jews with her, that He also wept (John 11:33-36).

The account of the Good Samaritan illustrates that compassion will compel us to action. *Jesus answering said, A*

The True Cross Bearers

certain man went down from Jerusalem to Jericho, and fell among thieves, which stripped him of his raiment, and wounded him, and departed, leaving him half dead. And by chance there came down a certain priest that way: and when he saw him, he passed by on the other side. And likewise a Levite, when he was at the place, came and looked on him, and passed by on the other side. But a certain Samaritan, as he journeyed, came where he was: and when he saw him, he had compassion on him, and went to him, and bound up his wounds, pouring in oil and wine, and set him on his own beast, and brought him to an inn, and took care of him. And on the morrow when he departed, he took out two pence, and gave them to the host, and said unto him, Take care of him; and whatsoever thou spendest more, when I come again, I will repay thee. Which now of these three, thinkest thou, was neighbour unto him that fell among the thieves? And he said, He that shewed mercy on him. Then said Jesus unto him, Go, and do thou likewise (Luke 10:30-37).

Compassion

We must be sensitive to the suffering and needs of others. We do not pass on the other side, but we make a difference. However, if we do not take up our cross daily and follow Christ, we will not be moved with compassion, nor will we seek to make a difference for others.

But I say unto you,
That ye resist not evil:
but whosoever shall smite thee
on the right cheek,
turn to him the other also.
(Matthew 5:39)

II. Resistance

Resistance: The act or power of resisting, opposing, or withstanding. The second step in being a true cross bearer is *resistance*. In many ways, resistance equals righteousness. **The key to doing right is to resist wrong.**

We must resist the temptation to do evil. In a world plagued with evil and a desire by so many to get even when wronged, it is easy to resist good and, in turn, do evil. Jesus says, *Whosoever shall smite thee on thy right cheek, turn to him the other also* (Matthew 5:39). In other words, do not respond in kind.

I know that if someone smites you, you will be tempted to set aside the Spirit within you and retaliate. If we do to others the same as they do to us, an eye for an eye, and a tooth for a tooth, what will we accomplish as His disciples? Is that the response of a cross bearer?

An eye for an eye leaves the whole world blind.
(M. K. Gandhi)

Scripture says that we should recompense to no man evil for evil, nor must we be overcome of evil but overcome evil with good. (See Romans 12:16-21.) We must resist every temptation to do evil. The enemy of our souls will do everything in his power to cause division between us. We must not yield to his temptations.

The apostle Paul wrote, *There hath no temptation taken you but such as is common to man, but . . . with the temptation [God will] also make a way of escape* (1 Corinthians 10:13). We will be tempted to do wrong. We will be tempted to get even. We will be tempted to lie, to cheat, and to steal. We will even be tempted to deny Christ, as did the apostle

Resistance

Peter (Luke 22:54-60). As some have already taken the bait, we will be tempted to lay down our cross and return to our old ways of life. We must realize that, with every temptation, there is always a way of escape. That escape is to stand firm upon the Word of God, take up our cross, deny our fleshly desires, and follow Him.

Resistance to do evil is a step toward righteousness. *For the fine linen is the righteousness of saints* (Revelation 19:8). **The cross can be borne only by those who have a heart for righteousness.** Those who are willing to carry it resist evil at all costs. If we are followers of Christ, we must realize the fruit of the Spirit entails goodness, righteousness, and truth. It would have been easy for the anointed David to respond in kind to King Saul. Instead, his response was: *The LORD forbid that I should stretch forth mine hand against the LORD'S anointed* (1 Samuel 26:11). We must turn the other cheek.

Who is a wise man and endued with knowledge among you? James asked. If we are endowed with the knowledge of

Christ, we must exhibit good behavior that shows our works performed with meekness by way of wisdom. We must not be overcome with bitterness, envy, or strife. Those things come not from above but are earthly, sensual, and devilish. For where envy and strife are, there are confusion and every evil work also. But the wisdom from above is first pure, then peaceable, gentle, easy to be entreated, full of mercy and good fruit, without partiality, and without hypocrisy. And the fruit of righteousness is sown in peace of them that make peace (my paraphrase). (See James 3:13-18.)

    We, who are anointed by the Lord and called to be cross bearers, must resist all temptation to do evil. **We must resist all forms of bigotry, selfishness, disunity, injustice, and inequality that hinder the truth of the gospel.** We must have the intestinal fortitude to walk away from evil, as well as the resolve and determination to do good to all men at all costs, especially to those who are of the household of faith. However, if we do not take up our cross daily and follow

Him, we will be tempted to respond as others who practice evil, injustice, inequality, and disunity, whose lives are centered upon themselves.

There is no temptation that we cannot resist. We have been given the power to tread over all the power of the enemy (Luke 10:19). We have the power to flee and to overcome sin. The cross reveals self-denial. We must deny ourselves, take up our cross daily, and follow Him.

Solomon stated that a good man is satisfied from himself (Proverbs 14:14). If we are Christ's servants, we are His free men. We must seek those things that make for peace. We must walk with a nonviolent approach to life. We must walk in the Spirit so we do not fulfill the lust of our flesh.

The apostle Peter explained our duty: *For even hereunto were ye called: because Christ also suffered for us, leaving us an example, that ye should follow his steps: who did no sin, neither was guile found in his mouth: who, when he was reviled, reviled not again; when he suffered, he threatened not; but committed himself to him that judgeth righteously: who his own self bare our sins in his own body on the tree, that we, being dead to sins, should live unto righteousness* (1 Peter 2:21-24).

There is no greater example of resistance to evil than Jesus Christ. We must learn from His example to do what is right and not what is evil. Resistance to evil, temptation, and wrong always shows strength of character in a man or woman who carries his or her cross daily and follows Jesus Christ.

***And being found in fashion
as a man,
he humbled himself,
and became obedient unto death,
even the death of the cross.***
(Philippians 2:8)

III. Obedience

Obedience: Submissive to the restraint or command of authority: willing to obey, the act of obeying; quality or state of being obedient. The third step in becoming a true cross bearer is *obedience*. "**Obedience, in human behavior, is a form of 'social influence in which a person yields to explicit instructions or orders from an authority figure**'" (Wikipedia). It is shown by self-discipline in one's ability to obey and to carry out the things which are asked of him. This attribute should be one of the first traits of character development in a person's life. Benjamin Franklin, one of the founding fathers of the United States, said, "Let the child's first lesson be obedience." Obedience should be the first lesson every parent teaches to his or her children . . . to obey.

The True Cross Bearers

One of the truest signs of one's love for God is obedience to His Word. The only way we can know if we are obeying Him is to know His Word. It is not possible for us to carry our cross if we do not obey and follow Him. If we call Him Lord, we must do what He says (Luke 6:46).

The trait of obedience is seen in one's life when that person does what he or she knows to do without being told. **Obedience is showing respect and submission to a greater authority.** It is carrying out the duties we have sworn to do. It calls for completing every task to the best of our ability. Obedience is more of a self-discipline trait than anything else.

Obedience reveals a heart that is in submission. Moses received a reprimand from God for smiting the rock when he was commanded to speak to the rock, thus preventing him from leading the children of Israel into the Promised Land. (See Numbers 20:7-13.) King Saul was also reprimanded by the prophet Samuel for his lack of obedience to God's commands when he sacrificed burnt offerings, a holy ritual he was not authorized to perform, and when he refused to destroy all the Amalekites as ordered. (See 1 Samuel 13; 15.) These actions set him in a place of divine disfavor and cost him his position as king.

Speaking of Abraham, the Lord said, *For I know him, that he will command his children and his household after him, and they shall keep the way of the LORD, to do justice and judgment; that the LORD may bring upon Abraham that which he hath spoken of him* (Genesis 18:19). By all accounts, Abraham was an obedient man. God told him to leave his home so that He could bless him, and Abraham obeyed (Genesis 12:1-3). God said he should offer his son Isaac, and he obeyed (Genesis 22:1-18).

Obedience requires one to keep going when his cross seems heavy. When others choose to do wrong, obedience says you must do what is right. When others say half an effort is good enough, obedience asks, "Would you be pleased if it was your own?"

The True Cross Bearers

Jesus was obedient to death, even the death of the cross. Although He prayed that the cup would pass from Him, He also prayed, *Nevertheless not my will, but thine, be done* (Luke 22:42). There will come a point of 'nevertheless' for cross bearers. No matter what it takes to maintain my obedience, I will obey and do. No one needs to force us to do it; we do it because we love Christ. Sometimes we have to swallow that bitter pill. **God's will is not always a pleasant trek up the hill.** We take up our cross because we are obedient to Him and His Word.

If we suffer because of our obedience while bearing our cross, the end state is still better than if we had refused it. A crown of life awaits us. Therefore, it is better if we willingly take the cross rather than being forced to bear it. God accepts only things done or given willingly, not grudgingly.

Notice, His obedience preceded Jesus in death. *And being found in fashion as a man, he humbled himself, and became obedient unto death, even the death of the cross*

Obedience

(Philippians 2:8). It went before Him. He was obedient and was willing to do what was right for one reason, even at the cost of His life. We were that one reason, so we could live. Sometimes obedience brings suffering, rejection, and loneliness. It can bring hate, envy, and even death as well.

The apostle James warned that we should be not only hearers of the Word of God but also doers of it so that we are not deceiving ourselves. The worst person one can deceive is himself. We must obey God's Word if we desire to be His true cross bearers.

As previously stated, obedience is an important character trait. Character is what makes us who we are. **Obedience is not something we dig up when it suits us or when we want to make others think well of us. It's a lifestyle.** It is only real if it is manifested daily. Our obedience to God and His principles must be consistent. We can see this with Abraham. Abraham could reason with God about Sodom and Gomorrah because he had first proven his obedience to God.

The True Cross Bearers

One who is not obedient to God cannot reason with God, as submission is required to gain favor with Him.

Sometimes we may suffer in our obedience to Him. *If we suffer [with him], we shall also reign with him* (2 Timothy 2:12). But Jesus offered us encouragement, *Blessed are ye, when men shall revile you, and persecute you, and shall say all manner of evil against you falsely, for my sake. Rejoice, and be exceeding glad: for great is your reward in heaven: for so persecuted they the prophets which were before you* (Matthew 5:11-12).

I have found the cross painful to bear sometimes. It can get heavy, particularly when there is a loss of a loved one, loneliness, a misunderstanding, or even outright rejection of one's good deeds. However, our obedience to God will help us pick up our cross daily and follow Him. Knowing this, our desire should be to please Him in all we do.

The writer of the book of Hebrews counseled, *Obey them that have the rule over you, and submit yourselves: for they watch for your souls, as they that must give account, that they may do it with joy, and not with grief: for that is unprofitable for you* (Hebrews 13:17). **We must have a heart of obedience because no man or woman is fit to lead anyone else unless he or she displays obedience.**

When we bear our cross, we will live above reproach and always do what is right no matter the cost. We must allow our obedience to go forth and be seen by all men.

***Submitting yourselves
one to another
in the fear of God.***
(Ephesians 5:21)

IV. Submission

Submission: To submit; to give over or yield to the power or authority of another; to subject oneself to another. The fourth step in being a true cross bearer is *submission*. Submission, like obedience, should be one of the first qualities of character developed in a person's life. Whereas obedience is knowing what to do and doing it without being told, submission is surrendering your will to the will of someone else and doing what you are being asked to do that is both ethically and morally right.

Why must we be submissive in order to be cross bearers? **Submission is an outward observance of an inward condition of the heart, indicating one's humility.** As one who is *called in the Lord, being a servant, is the Lord's* *freeman: likewise also he that is called, being free, is Christ's servant* (1 Corinthians 7:22).

Submission is not only a state of freedom but a heart to servanthood. When we submit to each other, we are willing to serve each other. A submarine is called a sub for short. The root prefix *sub* means "under." So when we submit, we are coming under another. If we are without a cross, we are not free nor under anyone but ourselves. We are still bound to our old way of life. This new life means we walk in newness of life. Once we hoist our cross upon our shoulders as Christ did upon His, we become free from self. If we will not submit to our spouse, our employer, our leaders, or our peers, we're not carrying our cross and we are not free. We cannot be submitted to Christ and not submitted to others.

Scripture says that we are to submit to one another in the fear of God (Ephesians 5:21). If we reverence God, we submit to God. And if we submit to God, we submit to every ethical and moral ordinance of man He places in our path. If we possess the mind of Christ, we must bear our cross. *Let this mind be in you, which was also in Christ Jesus: who, being in the form of God, thought it not robbery to be equal with God: but made himself of no reputation, and took upon him the form of a servant, and was made in the likeness of men: and being found in fashion as a man, he humbled himself, and became obedient unto death, even the death of the cross* (Philippians 2:5-8).

Because Jesus humbled and submitted Himself, He was exalted. Like Christ, those who submit prepare themselves for exaltation. *Likewise, ye younger,* Peter exhorted believers, *submit yourselves unto the elder. Yea, all of you be subject one to another, and be clothed with humility: for God resisteth the proud, and giveth grace to the humble. Humble yourselves therefore under the mighty hand of God, that he may exalt you in due time* (1 Peter 5:5-6).

True submission reveals one's state of humility more than anything else. **Submission does not mean that you are**

weak; instead, it's a sign of strength. It means you can set self aside and do what is asked. Peter also explained that we should be clothed with humility. **Even our outward appearance of humility should be a reflection of our inner heart of submission**. When we carry our cross, we submit to those over us and respect their position. If we stay on the low road, we'll find the high road that leads to life.

When thou art bidden of any man to a wedding, sit not down in the highest room; lest a more honourable man than thou be bidden of him; and he that bade thee and him come and say to thee, Give this man place; and thou begin with shame to take the lowest room. But when thou art bidden, go and sit down in the lowest room; that when he that bade thee cometh, he may say unto thee, Friend, go up higher: then shalt thou have worship in the presence of them that sit at meat with thee (Luke 14:8-10).

We must strive to serve others, and that service begins with submitting to the cross we are called to bear. We will not reflect Him before others if we are not submitted. If we are the Lord's free men and women, we must submit. Yea, *all of you be subject one to another,* Peter said. The Greek word for "subject" is *hoop-ot-as'-so*, which is to *subordinate*; reflexively, to *obey*: be under obedience (obedient), put under, subdue unto, (be, make) subject (to, unto), be (put) in subjection (to, under), submit self unto. Submit to one's control, to yield to one's admonition or advice.

The apostle said, "All of you be subject one to another." That's all of you. All of you is all of you. It includes everyone. No one is left out, excused, or excluded. It applies to Lottie, Dottie, and everybody. That means all! All the members of the church should submit themselves not only to their pastor but to fellow saints as well.

We should even submit to the superior rule of others, as we see with the centurion who came to Jesus, seeking for his servant's healing. He said, *For I am a man under authority* (Matthew 8:9). In other words, "I know how to submit to superior authority." We too must understand and follow the same rule and principle. **You can never be Christ's cross bearer if you do not submit to His authority.** We must not think more highly of ourselves than we ought.

As soon as they hear of me, they shall obey me: the strangers shall submit themselves unto me (Psalm 18:44). Note, people must hear of Him before they can obey Him and submit to Him. *For whosoever shall call upon the name of the Lord shall be saved. How then shall they call on him in whom they have not believed? and how shall they believe in him of whom they have not heard? and how shall they hear without a preacher? And how shall they preach, except they be sent? as it is written, How beautiful are the feet of them that preach the gospel of peace, and bring glad tidings of good things! But they have not all obeyed the gospel. For Esaias saith, Lord, who hath believed our report? So then faith cometh by hearing, and hearing by the word of God* (Romans 10:13-17).

Submission

True cross bearers are submitted servants carrying the gospel of Jesus Christ. They have already heard of Him, obeyed Acts 2:38, and submitted themselves to Him. They are chosen servants and witnesses that He is God (Isaiah 43:10-12). We who were at one time afar off and strangers are now made nigh by the blood of Jesus Christ (Ephesians 2:12-13). And now we who have heard—being born again, not of corruptible seed but of incorruptible, by the Word of God, which lives and abides forever—must obey and submit ourselves to the Lord Jesus and to each other, carry our cross daily, and make Him known.

*But Jesus called them unto him, and said,
Ye know that the princes of the Gentiles
exercise dominion over them,
and they that are great
exercise authority upon them.
But it shall not be so among you:
but whosoever will be chief among you,
let him be your servant:
even as the Son of man came
not to be ministered unto, but to minister,
and to give his life a ransom for many.*
(Matthew 20:25-28)

V. Servanthood

Servanthood: The condition of being a servant; placing the needs of others before self. The fifth step in being a true cross bearer is *servanthood*. According to Wikipedia, "Servant leadership is a leadership philosophy in which the main goal of the leader is to serve. This meaning is different from traditional leadership where the leader's main focus is the thriving of his company or organizations. A servant leader shares power, puts the needs of others first, and helps people develop and perform to the highest state possible." Instead of people's working to serve the leader, the leader exists for the purpose of serving the people. We see this in Jesus. **When true cross bearers shift their mind-set and serve first, they benefit, as do their followers.**

The True Cross Bearers

When we take up our cross, it requires service. God said through the prophet Isaiah, *Ye are my witnesses, saith the LORD, and my servant whom I have chosen: that ye may know and believe me, and understand that I am he: before me there was no God formed, neither shall there be after me* (Isaiah 43:10). We were chosen to serve and to make Him known.

Jesus told His disciples those who desire to be first must become the servants of all. Paul wrote his protege Timothy, *And the servant of the Lord must not strive; but be gentle unto all men, apt to teach, patient, in meekness instructing those that oppose themselves; if God peradventure will give them repentance to the acknowledging of the truth; and that they may recover themselves out of the snare of the devil, who are taken captive by him at his will* (2 Timothy 2:24-26).

True servanthood flows from the true cross bearer's heart of compassion and gentleness. It's a heart compacted with *agape* love. The Great Commission is a service mission. It is a call to go and serve. It's providing customer service, placing others before one's self. Jesus said He did not come to be ministered to but to minister (Matthew 20:28). Though He was King of kings and Lord of lords, the great and only Potentate, God manifested in flesh, He did not come for others to wait upon Him as natural kings and princes or those who see themselves as special or important do. He came to minister, to make others better. He came as a servant leader.

Jesus took on the form of a servant unto others and went from place to place doing good. Paul explained, *But made himself of no reputation, and took upon him the form of a servant, and was made in the likeness of men: and being found in fashion as a man, he humbled himself, and became obedient unto death, even the death of the cross* (Philippians 2:5-8). Such a servant leader was He: willing to wash others' feet, willing to cook a dinner of fish on the shore for His bewildered and weary disciples, willing to do whatever it took to make others better, even willing to die that others may live. Not until we take up our cross daily can we serve like Him.

The True Cross Bearers

For I have given you an example, that ye should do as I have done to you. Verily, verily, I say unto you, The servant is not greater than his lord; neither he that is sent greater than he that sent him. If ye know these things, happy are ye if ye do them, Jesus said (John 13:15-17). Happy you will be if you serve. It is a joy to serve others. But without a cross on our shoulders, we will always want others to serve us. **Find me a Christian not willing to serve, and I will show you one without a cross.** It's become too heavy for him; he has become weak in the faith, fainthearted, self-serving. He has forgotten the servant is not greater than his Lord. Without a cross, our view of servanthood will be a worldly one, not a spiritual one. Jesus has given us an example of a true cross bearer, portraying true servanthood.

A servant leader shares power, empowers others, puts the needs of others first, and helps people develop and perform as highly as possible. Jesus shared with us His power (Luke 10:19; Acts 2:1-4). He empowered us. He has placed our needs before His. *For scarcely for a righteous man will one die: yet peradventure for a good man some would even dare to die. But God commendeth his love toward us, in that, while we were yet sinners, Christ died for us* (Romans 5:7-8). He carried His cross, and now we must carry ours if we say that we are His servants. We must now share His power and place the needs of others before ours, as we help them grow and perform to the highest level of spiritual development.

Notice the charge Jesus gave us. *Go ye therefore, and teach all nations, baptizing them in the name of the Father, and of the Son, and of the Holy Ghost: teaching them to observe all things whatsoever I have commanded you: and, lo, I am with you alway, even unto the end of the world. Amen* (Matthew 28:19-20).

To be a true cross bearer, we must have a servant's heart. The apostle Paul's first question when he met Jesus on the road to Damascus was: "Who art thou, Lord?" His second question was: "Lord, what wilt thou have me to do?" Paul

The True Cross Bearers

seemed to grasp that revelation required service. Revelation equals transformation. **True cross bearers are transformed to serve.** We must love Him and serve Him. We should not think more highly of ourselves than we ought, but we should think soberly because God has done the work in us.

We should not think that our gifting, abilities, enlightenment of the gospel, and the knowledge of Christ we have been given are of ourselves. They are from God, given so we may serve others and become true cross bearers. We should never think of ourselves as superior. We are servants of the Lord. The first must be last. We must be willing to bear our cross and to place others before us. We must all understand protocol and respect. **But the true cross bearer prefers others better than himself or herself.**

The story of the Good Samaritan (Luke 10:30-37) is the narrative of a true cross bearer. Although the man had been beaten half to death and left to die and though others walked by, saw him, and left him in that state, the Samaritan was moved with compassion to help. He displayed service before self. His responses showed the true cross bearer in action.

Jesus, humbling Himself, taking on the form and duties of a servant, wearing a towel, and washing His disciples' feet, showed us how true servant leadership looks. He was what humility looked like. He was what servanthood truly is. That's what true cross bearers and followers after Him must look like.

But which of you, Jesus said, *having a servant plowing or feeding cattle, will say unto him by and by, when he is come from the field, Go and sit down to meat? And will not rather say unto him, Make ready wherewith I may sup, and gird thyself, and serve me, till I have eaten and drunken; and afterward thou shalt eat and drink? Doth he thank that servant because he did the things that were commanded him? I trow not. So likewise ye, when ye shall have done all those things which are commanded you, say, We are unprofitable servants: we have done that which was our duty to do* (Luke

17:7-10). Our ultimate duty calls us to do the things He has commanded us to do and to serve others.

To be His true cross bearers, we must have compassion and make a difference in others' lives. We must resist every temptation to do evil. We must live a lifestyle of total obedience to Jesus and His Word while being submitted to one another in the fear of God. Lastly, we must have a servant's heart so we can fulfill the Great Commission. But to fulfill His commission, we must daily take up our cross and follow Him; otherwise, we can never be His disciples.

Are you a true cross bearer?

9780757760914